Paint a Sun in the Sky
A First Look at the Seasons

by Claire Llewellyn   illustrated by Amanda Wood

Thanks to our reading adviser:

Susan Kesselring, M.A., Literacy Educator
Rosemount-Apple Valley-Eagan (Minnesota) School District

PICTURE WINDOW BOOKS
Minneapolis, Minnesota

First American edition published in 2005 by
Picture Window Books
5115 Excelsior Boulevard
Suite 232
Minneapolis, MN 55416
877-845-8392
www.picturewindowbooks.com

First Published in Great Britain in 1999 by Macdonald Young Books,
an imprint of Wayland Publishers Ltd.
61 Western Road
Hove
East Sussex
BN3 1JD

Text copyright © Claire Llewellyn 1999
Illustrations copyright © Amanda Wood 1999
Volume copyright © Macdonald Young Books 1999

Printed in the United States of America.

Library of Congress Cataloging-in-Publication Data
Llewellyn, Claire.
Paint a sun in the sky : a first look at the seasons / by Claire
Llewellyn ; illustrated by Amanda Wood.
p. cm. — (First look : science)
ISBN 1-4048-0659-8
1. Seasons—Juvenile literature. I. Wood, Amanda, ill. II. Title.
III. Series.
QB637.L65 2005
508.2—dc22   2004007313

To Anna and Owen – C.L.
For Todd and all his friends in Miss Perryman's class – A.W.

Spring blossoms open, and flowers

shoot up through the chilly ground.

7

In come T-shirts, caps, and shorts.

In early autumn, nuts, berries, apples,

and pears ripen on bushes and trees.

17

Soon the leaves on the trees change color

In winter, the sun is low in the sky.

20

The days are short and cold.

The best winter days have

bright sunshine and snow.

make the picture of the year.

A sun in the sky!

Why do we have seasons?

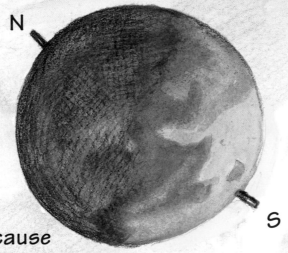

In December, the South Pole leans toward the sun. The south has summer. The north has winter.

We have seasons because of the way Earth moves around the sun. This journey is called Earth's orbit, and it takes exactly one year.

Earth isn't upright as it orbits the sun. It's tilted to one side. So, at different times on its journey, first one pole and then the other leans toward the sun. This is why we have seasons.

In March, neither pole leans toward the sun, but the south is getting cooler (autumn), and the north is warming up (spring).

In September, neither pole leans toward the sun, but it's getting warmer in the south (spring) and cooler in the north (autumn).

In June, the North Pole leans toward the sun. The north has summer. The south has winter.

Useful Words

Blossom
Small flowers that open on trees in spring.

Nectar
The sweet juice inside a flower.

Orbit
The pathway of Earth as it moves around the sun.

Pole
The name given to the most northern and most southern parts of Earth.

Season
A part of the year that has its own sort of weather.

Fun Facts

- If you live north of the equator, you see the most sunlight on June 21, which is the first day of summer.

- You see the least sunlight on December 21, which is the first day of winter.

- It takes about eight minutes for the sun's light to hit Earth.

- Earth is closest to the sun in January.

- The sun is about 93 million miles (149 million kilometers) from Earth.

To Learn More

At the Library

Bradley, Franklyn M. *Sunshine Makes the Seasons*. New York: HarperCollins, 2005.
Gibbons, Gail. *The Reasons for Seasons*. New York: Holiday House, 1996.
Warren, Jean. *Four Seasons: Science*. Everett, Wash.: Warren Pulishing House, 1996.

On the Web

FactHound offers a safe, fun way to find Web sites related to this book. All of the sites on FactHound have been researched by our staff. www.facthound.com

1. Visit the FactHound home page.
2. Enter a search word related to this book, or type in this special code: 1404806598.
3. Click the FETCH IT button.

Your trusty FactHound will fetch the best Web sites for you!

Index

Look for all the books in this series:

A Seed in Need
A First Look at the Plant Cycle

And Everyone Shouted, "Pull!"
A First Look at Forces of Motion

From Little Acorns ...
A First Look at the Life Cycle of a Tree

Paint a Sun in the Sky
A First Look at the Seasons

Take a Walk on a Rainbow
A First Look at Color

The Case of the Missing Caterpillar
A First Look at the Life Cycle of a Butterfly

The Drop Goes Plop
A First Look at the Water Cycle

The Hen Can't Help It
A First Look at the Life Cycle of a Chicken

The Trouble with Tadpoles
A First Look at the Life Cycle of a Frog